Proven methods for

DOUBLING YOUR $ALARY

in 90 days or less

Proven methods for

DOUBLING YOUR $ALARY

in 90 days or less

Pooja Singhal

360⁰ Cloud Consulting From Every Angle

Worldwide Published by

Pendown Press

PENDOWN PRESS LLP

An ISO 9001 & ISO 14001 Certified Co.,

Regd. Office: 3767A, Kanhaiya Nagar,

Tri Nagar, Delhi-110035

Ph.: 8130886000, 9650072927, 8595249536

E-mail: info@pendownpress.com

Branch Office: 1A/2A, 20, Hari Sadan, Ansari Road,

Daryaganj, New Delhi-110002

Ph.: 011-45794768

Website: PendownPress.com

First Edition: 2023

Price: ₹399/-

ISBN: 978-93-5554-963-1

Layout and Cover Designed by Pendown Graphics Team
Printed and Bound in India by Thomson Press India Ltd.

Contents

1 90 Day Challenge

Your Next 90 Days

While earning a high salary is a dream for many people, it's not uncommon for individuals to seek ways to increase their income quickly.

In this mini-book, we will discuss how to double your salary in just 90 days.

Step 1: Evaluate Your Skills

Before embarking on a journey to double your salary, evaluate your skills. Make a list of your skills and compare them with the skills required for higher-paying jobs. If there's a mismatch, work on acquiring the necessary skills. Take up courses or certifications that will enhance your skills and make you more valuable to employers.

Step 2: Network

Networking is vital for career growth - attend industry events, conferences; connect with other professionals in your field; build relationships with people who can help you advance your career. You never know who might have a job opportunity that aligns with your career goals.

Step 3: Leverage Your Current Role

Your current role can help you increase your salary. Speak to your manager about taking on additional responsibilities or projects that align with your career goals. Showcase your accomplishments and discuss your future career plans. If your company has a performance-based bonus program, make sure you understand how it works and what you need to do to achieve it.

Step 4: Apply for Higher Paying Jobs

If you're looking to increase your salary quickly, apply for higher-paying jobs. Look for job postings that align with your skills and experience. Tailor your resume and cover letter to each job application. Practice your interview skills and prepare for any potential questions that might arise.

Step 5: Negotiate Your Salary

When you receive a job offer, negotiate your salary. Research the average salary range for the position in your area. Consider your skills and experience when deciding on a salary range to negotiate. Remember that negotiating your salary can make a long-term impact on your future earnings.

The Verdict?

Doubling your salary in 90 days is achievable but requires effort and dedication.

By evaluating your skills, networking, leveraging your current role, applying for higher-paying jobs, and negotiating your salary, you can increase your income and reach your career goals.

Remember that patience and persistence are key, and with hard work, you can achieve success. Employers wish to see evidence of dedication.

2 Some Life-Changing Stories by REAL DEVELOPERS and SALESPEOPLE

Tenfold Increase in 3 Years

"Hi, I'm Monika, and I'm excited to share my journey with 360 Degree Cloud Technologies. When I joined the company three years ago, my starting salary was 3.0 Lacs, and I was thrilled to be part of such a dynamic and innovative team.

Over the years, I've had the opportunity to work on various projects and develop my skills, which have been recognized and rewarded by the company. My hard work and dedication have been acknowledged with salary hikes and promotions, and I'm proud to say that my salary has increased tenfold in just three years.

360 Degree Cloud Technologies has provided me with a supportive work environment where I have been encouraged to learn and grow. The company's focus on innovation and excellence has enabled me to work on cutting-edge technologies and projects, which have challenged me to push my limits and excel in my role.

I am grateful for the opportunities that 360 Degree Cloud Technologies has given me, and I look forward to continuing my journey with the company. The growth and success that I have achieved here have been unparalleled, and I would recommend anyone looking for a fulfilling career in the IT industry to consider joining this dynamic and innovative team."

Life-Changing Incentives

"Hi, I'm Khushboo, a Salesperson at 360 Degree Cloud. I have been in the sales industry for over seven years and have worked with various organizations, but nothing compares to what I've experienced here. 360 Degree Cloud is a sales-driven company that values its employees' efforts and rewards them accordingly. The company provides its sales team with all the necessary tools and resources to excel in their roles, including comprehensive training programs, innovative technology, and a supportive work environment.

What sets 360 Degree Cloud apart from other organizations is its unique incentive structure. As a salesperson, I have the opportunity to earn a substantial amount of incentives, which are directly tied to my performance. The company recognizes and rewards hard work, and this has motivated me to go above and beyond in my role. During my time at 360 Degree Cloud, I have achieved significant sales milestones, and the incentives I have earned have been life-changing. This has given me the financial stability to pursue my personal goals and live the life I have always wanted.

I am grateful for the opportunity to work with such a dynamic and innovative company that values its employees and provides them with the tools and resources they need to succeed. If you are looking for a career in sales, I highly recommend joining 360 Degree Cloud. The incentives, coupled with the company's supportive work culture, make it an ideal place to build a rewarding career."

Growing with a Clear Career Track as a Developer

"Hello, I'm Shivam, and I have been working as a Salesforce Developer at 360 Degree Cloud for the past five years. I am excited to share my journey with the company and thrilled to be celebrating this milestone.

When I joined 360 Degree Cloud five years ago, I was looking for a company that would provide me with challenging work and opportunities to learn and grow in my role. While I have friends who work at different Salesforce companies, I can confidently say that the kind of learning and exposure I have had here is unbeatable.

360 Degree Cloud has provided me with an excellent platform to explore various Salesforce clouds and work on projects that have challenged me to expand my skill set. I have worked on

Sales, Service, Marketing, Velocity, and CPQ clouds, and the learning doesn't stop here. The company has invested in comprehensive training programs, and I have been able to stay up-to-date with the latest trends and technologies in the Salesforce ecosystem.

What I love most about 360 Degree Cloud is the company's focus on innovation and its supportive work environment. The company encourages its employees to come up with innovative solutions to complex problems and recognizes and rewards hard work.

During my five years with the company, I have had the opportunity to work on various projects, including some high-profile ones, which have given me invaluable experience and exposure. I am grateful for the opportunities that 360 Degree Cloud has given me, and I look forward to continuing my journey with the company.

If you are looking for a company that provides challenging work, excellent learning opportunities, and a supportive work environment, I highly recommend joining 360 Degree Cloud. The experience I have had here is unparalleled, and I am confident that you will have a similar experience."

Financing Personal Goals

"Hi there! My name is Kumar Madhurendra, and I've been with 360 Degree Cloud for six years now. Throughout my time with the company, I've been given countless opportunities to grow and develop my career in ways that I never thought possible.

As a Senior Salesforce Developer and Tech Lead, I currently lead a team of 40 developers, which is a testament to the trust and support that the company has placed in me.

One of the things that truly sets 360 Degree Cloud apart from other companies is its unwavering commitment to recognizing and rewarding hard work. As a developer, I understand how challenging it can be to earn a good salary at this stage of your career. However, at 360 Degree Cloud, this is not an issue. The company understands the value that developers bring to the table and compensates them accordingly.

The incentives are substantial, and they've made a significant impact on my finances. This has allowed me to live the life I've always wanted and pursue my personal goals.

360 Degree Cloud also provides its employees with a supportive work environment that encourages innovation and growth. The company invests in comprehensive training programs and provides the latest tools and technologies to help employees excel in their roles.

If you're a Senior Developer or Tech Lead like me and you're looking for a company that values hard work and provides a supportive work culture, I highly recommend joining 360 Degree Cloud. The incentives, coupled with the company's supportive work culture, make it an ideal place to build a rewarding career."

3 Shake Hands with Us

360 Degree Cloud is a rapidly growing Salesforce boutique company that specializes in providing top-notch Salesforce solutions to clients worldwide. As a Salesforce Platinum Partner, the company is widely recognized for its premium AppExchange product called 360 SMS App, which has received global recognition. Recently, the company launched a new product called 360 CTI for Salesforce Phone Calling, generating significant interest in the market.

The company has a team of skilled Salesforce developers, architects, consultants, and quality analysts who work tirelessly to deliver high-quality projects and products to its enterprise-level clients. With over 3000 clients across the globe, the company employs over 600 professionals in Pan India and has branches in Pune, Kolkata, Noida, Faridabad, and Meerut. The company has received several accolades, including being recognized as the Best Salesforce Consulting Company of 2022 by Business Connect Magazine.

The company aims to expand its reach across all Salesforce niche skills, including Velocity, DevOps, CPQ, and Marketing Cloud. To achieve this goal, it is looking to hire experienced Salesforce professionals who are willing to contribute to the company's growth and expansion.

360 Degree Cloud offers exciting opportunities for both tech and non-tech roles, and its testimonials prove that it pays more than the market figures. If you're looking for a job change, you can share your resume with hr@360degreecloud.com.

Alternatively, you can partner with the company in selling its products or refer someone to the company and earn a high commission. For instance, 360 CTI is an easy-to-use CTI app that seamlessly integrates with Salesforce, allowing your clients to make calls directly from their CRM. DEVELOPERS EARN UP TO 15% REFERRAL WHEN THEY IMPLEMENT 360 CTI FOR A CLIENT.

To know more about how to earn by selling the company's CTI application (360 CTI), scan the QR code below:

Parting Words

In conclusion, doubling your salary in just 90 days may be a challenging goal, but it's not impossible.

With a focused mindset, determination, and hard work, you can achieve this feat. Throughout this book, we've discussed several strategies and tips that can help you achieve your financial goals.

These include developing your skills, building your personal brand, networking, and negotiating your salary.

However, keep in mind that achieving your financial goals is not just about the money; it's also about your personal growth and job satisfaction. Therefore, continue to learn, take calculated risks, and seize opportunities that come your way. We hope that this book has been a valuable resource for you, and we encourage you to implement the strategies discussed here to achieve your desired income level.

Good luck on your journey to doubling your salary!

Proven methods for DOUBLING YOUR SALARY in 90 days or less

Are you tired of living paycheck to paycheck?

Do you dream of doubling your salary? This mini-book is for you.

In just five steps, you will learn how to evaluate your skills, network, leverage your current role, apply for higher-paying jobs, and negotiate your salary. With dedication and effort, you too can increase your income and reach your career goals.

Three successful professionals at 360 Degree Cloud Technologies also share their stories of career growth:

Monika increased her salary tenfold in three years as a software engineer; Khushboo achieved significant sales milestones and earned life-changing incentives as a salesperson; and Shivam had opportunities to learn and grow as a Salesforce developer.

Join these successful professionals and start your journey to doubling your salary today.

About The Author

Pooja Singhal, MD of 360 Degree Cloud, is an entrepreneur and business professional with 14+ years of experience as a business strategist.

She excels in developing sales and marketing strategies, driving innovation and differentiation, and exceeding revenue goals.

Reach out to us at
contact@360degreecloud.com
or call us at +91 806 902 7850.

NOTES:

NOTES:

NOTES:

NOTES:

NOTES:

NOTES:

NOTES: ✍

NOTES:

NOTES:

NOTES: ✍